THE ANCIENT
INDIANS

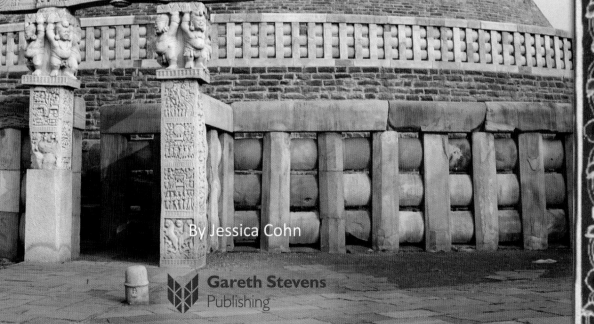

By Jessica Cohn

Gareth Stevens
Publishing

Please visit our website, www.garethstevens.com. For a free color catalog of all our high-quality books, call toll free 1-800-542-2595 or fax 1-877-542-2596.

Library of Congress Cataloging-in-Publication Data
Cohn, Jessica.
The ancient Indians / Jessica Cohn.
   p. cm. — (Crafts from the past)
 Includes bibliographical references and index.
ISBN 978-1-4339-7719-0 (pbk.)
ISBN 978-1-4339-7720-6 (6-pack)
ISBN 978-1-4339-7718-3 (library binding)
1. India—Civilization—To 1200—Juvenile literature. 2. India—History—To 324 B.C.—Juvenile literature. 3. India History—324 B.C.-1000 A.D.—Juvenile literature. 4. India—Social life and customs—To 1200—Juvenile literature. 5. Handicraft—India—Juvenile literature. I. Title.

 DS425.C5835 2013
 934—dc23

2012006828

First Edition
Published in 2013 by
Gareth Stevens Publishing
111 East 14th Street, Suite 349
New York, NY 10003

© 2013 Gareth Stevens Publishing

Produced by Netscribes Inc.
Art Director Dibakar Acharjee
Editorial Content The Wordbench
Copy Editor Dorothy Anderson
Picture Researcher Sandeep Kumar G
Designer Ravinder Kumar
Illustrators Ashish Tanwar, Indranil Ganguly, Prithwiraj Samat and Rohit Sharma

Photo credits:
t = top, a = above, b = below, l = left, r = right, c = center
Front Cover: Netscribes Inc., Shutterstock Images LLC Title Page: Shutterstock Images LLC
Contents Page: Shutterstock Images LLC Inside: Netscribes Inc.: 5b, 7tl, 7tr, 7bl, 7br, 10, 11tl, 11tr, 11bl, 11br, 15tl, 15tr, 15bl, 15br, 19tl, 19tr, 19bl, 19br, 23tl, 23tr, 23bl, 23br, 27tl, 27tr, 27bl, 27br, 31tl, 31tr, 31bl, 31br, 35t, 35c, 35b, 38, 39tl, 39tr, 39bl, 39br Dreamstime: 33b, 42l Shutterstock Images LLC: 5t, 6t, 6b, 8, 9, 12, 13, 14t, 14b, 16, 17, 18, 20, 21t, 21b, 22t, 22b, 24, 25, 26, 28, 29, 30l, 30r, 32, 33t, 34, 36t, 36b, 37, 40, 41, 42r, 43tl, 43tr, 48b Thinkstock: 4

Printed in the United States of America

CPSIA compliance information: Batch #CS12GS: For further information contact Gareth Stevens, New York, New York at 1-800-542-2595.

Contents

A Great Land

Long ago, people settled along the Indus River and its **tributaries**. The ancient people built settlements on land that is now part of Pakistan and western India. More than a thousand related sites have been found. These remains tell an astounding story. The people in the Indus valley formed the largest of the first civilizations.

The large towns of the Indus valley civilization were laid out with streets in rectangular patterns.

4

City Water

Their biggest towns were on the largest rivers.
Mohenjo-daro was on the Indus River. Harappa
was on the Ravi River. In this advanced society,
the people had brick homes and water drains.
Their settlements were at their height from
2500 B.C. to 1900 B.C. Then this early civilization
mysteriously disappeared.

It appears that there were more than
5 million people in the Indus valley
civilization. It is not known for certain
whether they had one culture.

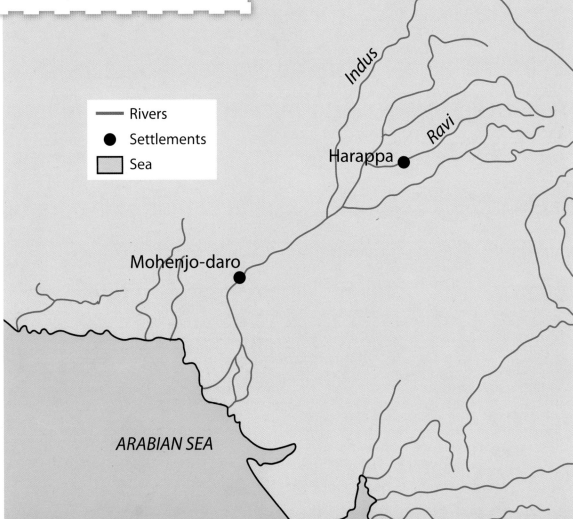

Rivers
Settlements
Sea

Indus

Ravi

Harappa

Mohenjo-daro

ARABIAN SEA

Into India

Some of the people from this early society may have moved eastward. In the years that followed, other settlements on the **subcontinent** expanded. The land that is now India was further developed. The population grew. People known as the Indo-Aryans moved into India from the northwest.

देवानंपिमे पियदसि लाजा
हेवं आहा
या इयं धंमेन पालना धंमेन
विघाने धंमेन सुखियना धंमेन
गोती ति
कियबु धंमेनि अपासिनवे
बहुकायानि दयादाने सचे सोबये
एकंबि भंते भगवता बुधन
भासिते सवे से सुभासिते वा
मंगोसंपि मे निगोहानि लोघापितानि
छायोपगानि होसंति पसुमुनिसान
अंबाबडिक्या लोपापिता अटंकोसिक्य
निपिमे उदुपानानि खनापापितानि

Up

Many of the beliefs and traditions of the early people of India were captured in the **Vedas**, the oldest texts of the time. The Vedas include stories that give people ways to think about life. One early text talks about dawn as the head of a horse. Its eye is the sun. Its body is the year. Heaven is its back. Space is its belly, and Earth is the underbelly.

The people may have left the earlier settlements because rivers changed course. Or there may have been a drought.

Horsing Around

In the Vedas, horses are symbols of energy. In that spirit, you can make a horse that is powered by imagination.

Materials Needed

- Large solid-colored sock with bent heel
- Pillow stuffing or old newspapers
- Fabric markers
- Felt and yarn scraps
- Scissors
- Sewing needle, thread
- Optional: an adult to help with sewing
- Stick, such as an old curtain rod
- Thick rubber band

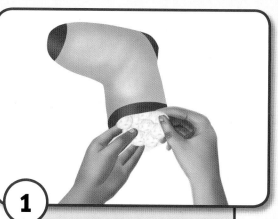

1 Fill the sock with stuffing. Then draw eyes near the sock's heel and nostrils and a mouth near its toe.

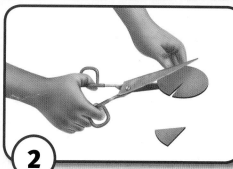

2 Cut two triangles of felt for ears, and sew them in place near the heel. Cut yarn or felt for a mane, if you want, or just draw it on.

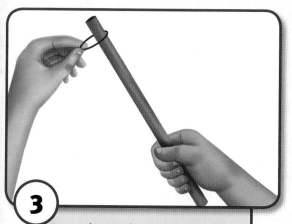

3 Now, loop the rubber band around one end of the stick so it stays in place, but you can still stretch it.

4 Push the banded end of the stick into the open end of the sock. Stretch the band over the end of the sock, and get ready to ride or put on a puppet show.

Gifts of the Ganges

Much of the land in south Asia was fertile. In addition to rice and other foods, the people grew cotton for clothing. Their times to plant and harvest were determined by the **monsoons**. These major wind shifts brought heavy rains. The rains built up the Ganges and other waterways and made two growing seasons possible.

Three-quarters of the farmland in India is still used to grow cereal grains.

Digging In

Ancient India was rich with raw materials. The land had large deposits of stones, such as granite, that were used for buildings. The early people also dug for useful metals. The first civilization in the Indus valley made tools from **bronze**. During the **Iron Age**, which followed, the people learned to use and shape iron.

In an old Vedic story about a god who ends a drought, the god rides a white elephant when he frees the rain clouds from a cave.

Iron Rule

During the Iron Age, the settlements in India were united under the rule of the Mauryan **dynasty**. The Mauryas started their kingdom in the East, in about 323 B.C. As they pushed their way west, the Mauryas made rules to protect the forests and the animals. They studied the soils and built dams, which helped the farmers and the cities.

The Mauryas ruled one of the largest empires of the time.

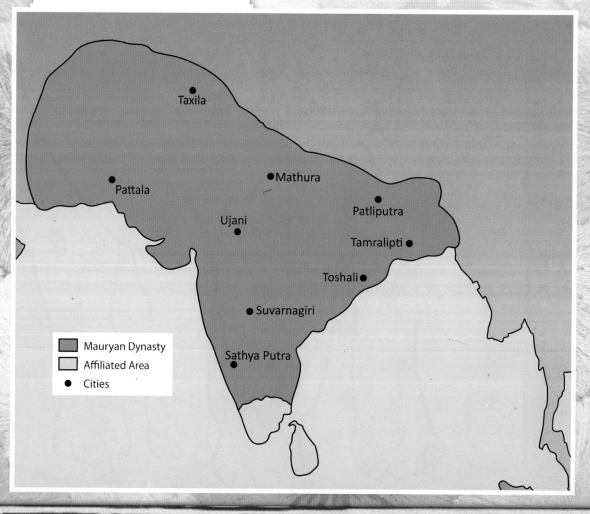

Taxila

Pattala

Mathura

Ujani

Patliputra

Tamralipti

Toshali

Suvarnagiri

Sathya Putra

Mauryan Dynasty
Affiliated Area
• Cities

Cotton Into Wool

People in India have grown cotton and raised sheep for wool for thousands of years. None of them were able to manage this trick, though. Here is a way to turn cotton into "wool."

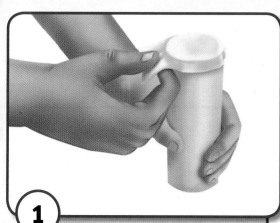

1 Cover both ends of the toilet paper tube with masking tape.

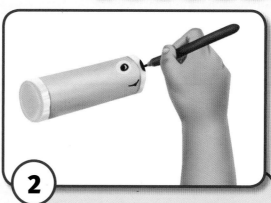

2 Pick one end to be your sheep's face. Glue the eyes in place, and draw a nose and mouth.

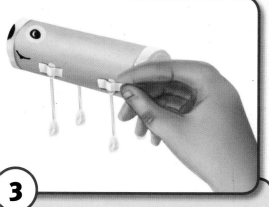

3 Now, your sheep needs legs. Tape cotton swabs to the sides of the tube so they stick out like legs.

4 Go crazy with the glue and cotton balls. Cover everything except the face. The more tightly you pack the cotton balls, the warmer your sheep's "wool" will be.

Sense of Belonging

The early society had four basic divisions, known as the **caste system**. The priests were at the top. Service workers were at the bottom. The communities that people were born into were their **jatis**. By tradition, a person was supposed to marry within his or her group. A boy was expected to do the work of his father.

The priests and scholars were at the top. Then came warriors and rulers. They were followed by people in commerce, such as farmers and merchants. Then came service workers. There was also a lower class, the members of which were known as "untouchables." They did dirty work no one else wanted to do.

Rules of the Pack

In south Asian society, the people considered the needs of their group rather than just themselves. The jatis had rules that members followed. The rules related to how a person acted. They discussed subjects such as what someone could eat and what was expected when doing certain jobs.

Holy men break their attachments to society and material goods. This is considered the "fourth stage" of life.

Front of the Class

The social system was set in some ways, but the jatis had ways to improve their status. For example, the local traders brought food and raw materials to the cities. The sea traders exchanged goods and services over great distances. Many successful traders were able to buy land and lend money. Their jatis became more powerful, despite their caste.

Local trade took place in open-air markets, which operate today in much the same way.

Close-Up

Fast-forward to the future. Today, there are thousands of jatis in India. Each jati is associated with one kind of job, but some jati members do other kinds of work. It is illegal to discriminate against untouchables.

Setting the Standard

The ancient Indians developed the use of **standard weights** and an elaborate system of weights and measures. Now, you can try it on your own scale.

Materials Needed
- Plastic hanger
- Drinking straw
- Glue
- String
- Scissors
- Five paper clips
- Two identical paper cups
- Hole puncher

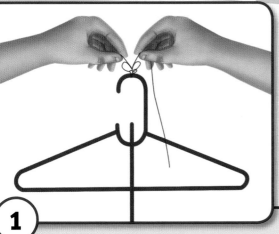

1 Glue the straw to the hanger, right down the middle. Then, tie a long string to the hanger's hook.

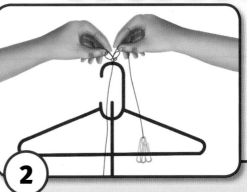

2 Tie another string, 10 inches long, around the paper clips, and then tie the other end to the hook, over the first knot. This is the **plumb bob**.

3 Punch two holes across from each other on each cup, near the rim. Cut two 10-inch strings. Tie the exact middle of each around the two corners of the hanger. Tie the ends to the two holes in each cup.

4 Hang the "scale" by the original string. It should hang straight and not touch anything. The plumb bob should hang freely. Now, when you put objects in the cups, the straw will point to the side that is lighter.

Abundant Beliefs

The early people in the Indus valley made seals showing animals and other figures. The seals seem to have to do with religion, but it is hard to know. No one can read the writing from that time. What is known about religion in the region came later, when India's culture bloomed. The spiritual beliefs that blossomed then include **Hinduism**, **Buddhism**, and **Jainism**.

In Hindu thinking, "maya" is the name for the things people can perceive with the senses. Maya is not supposed to be trusted.

In the Spirit

The word "Hindu" is an English label for many spiritual practices found in India. Hinduism teaches that people cause the bad and good that happen. Its practices encourage people to escape lesser fates through better understanding. The traditions cover many things, from the acts of priests to how people should treat houseguests.

Yoga features mindful body movement and breath. Its practice is part of Hindu traditions.

Many Paths

Jainism arose from the Indus valley. The core of this religion is the belief in nonviolence. Buddhism was begun in northern India. The Buddha was a teacher who was born around 563 B.C. Among his main teachings was the belief that suffering leads to rebirth. He taught that a person's deeds are rewarded, for better or worse.

The word "Buddha" means the "enlightened one."

Close-Up

The Buddha was a man named Siddhartha Gautama. He was born into a royal family. At the age of 29, he left his fancy home and crossed the countryside, looking for meaning in life. He discovered new ways of thinking, went through an awakening, and became a teacher.

Making Your Mark

The Indus valley seals were probably used to mark things the way we use signatures or stamps today. Each one would have made a unique impression in clay. Now, what's your impression?

Materials Needed
- Small bar of soap
- Empty ink pen
- Modeling clay

1

Decide what you want your seal to have on it. Remember, it's a stamp, so any writing has to be done backward to come out forward.

2

Use the pen to scratch your image into the flat side of the bar of soap. Try to dig in. Shallow or very thin lines will not show up well.

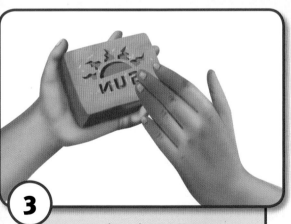

3

Use your hands to wipe any excess soap scraps off the bar. Now, you have your seal.

4

Roll the clay into a ball. With the image side down, stamp your seal into the clay. Pull back the seal, and see how your image comes out.

On the Mountains

The early worshippers built enormous temples by cutting into caves. About 1,200 of these awesome structures have been found. In the north, near the village of Ajanta, are the Ajanta Caves. Some were used as **sanctuaries**. Others served as **monasteries** for Buddhist monks.

The paintings on the walls at the Ajanta Caves tell Buddhist stories.

Sacred Sites

The Mauryan dynasty set up pillars that listed religious beliefs. The pillars were made of wood at first. At the end of the dynasty, the pillars were stonework. The people of that time also built **burial mounds**. As time went on, the people made sacred buildings shaped like mounds. These structures were called **stupas**. They housed sacred items.

The pillar at Sarnath was built by the last Mauryan emperor and is now the state symbol of India.

The Great Stupa was built just before or after 100 B.C.

Brick by Brick

In the early Indus valley culture, the homes were made of bricks. The buildings had flat roofs and were built around courtyards. Even then, the homes had private baths and more than one story. The early cities featured public baths, **granaries**, and large town walls for protection.

Citadels remained a key part of later structures, such as Kumbhalgarh fort, which was started in the 15th century.

Close-Up

The ancient cities were guarded by **citadels**, which were walled structures on high ground. Were they used to protect people from attacks? Did they have meaning for religious ceremonies? Did they hold back floods? It is not known for certain.

The early Indus valley people made designs that they thought were magical. This custom was carried on in India as a type of folk art called **rangoli**.

Marked for Luck

In India, rangoli markings are placed near the door for celebrations. The designs feature fish, flowers, and other elements. The artists might fill in their designs with flower petals or rice powder for color, but you can fill in yours using paint.

Materials Needed
- Grid paper or plain paper
- Pencil
- Paint and paintbrush

1 If not using grid paper, draw a grid of light, evenly spaced dots. For the first try, keep the dots in square rows.

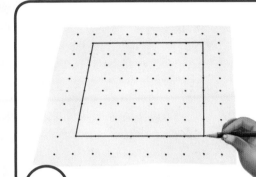

2 Plan your design as a square or circle. You will want to fill the space with a pattern that looks "even" from side to side.

3 Once you have your idea ready, go ahead and draw a line. Repeat the process until you have a design you like.

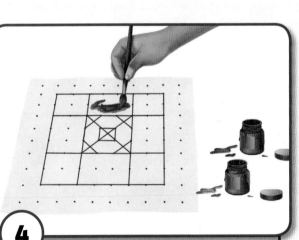

4 Now, color in the spaces between your lines. By tradition, a gap is a space for evil spirits to enter!

Great Grains

Many thousands of years ago, the early people of India grew wheat, barley, and dates. Mangoes and muskmelons grew naturally. As time went on, the farmers filled fields with cotton and **hemp** to make clothing. The people harvested wild rice and then learned to grow it. Wild fields of sugarcane led to the development of sugar.

Rice was often eaten with curds of milk or yogurt in ancient times.

Double Harvest

Each year brought two monsoons, which led to two harvests. The farmers irrigated the fields to make the most of the water. In the cities, there were granaries where the harvested grains could be stored. The people kept cows, pigs, buffalo, and sheep.

The ancient Indians first wrote about animal medicine and care in the Vedas.

Meal Making

Early in history, the main meal was some kind of cereal and some kind of fish or meat. The Vedas talk about fried barley and crushed grains. They mention a kind of cake. The ancient texts discuss milk, milk curds, and **ghee**, which is a form of butter. After Buddhism became popular, more people ate **vegetarian** meals.

Sugarcane is a kind of tall grass that is native to south Asia.

Close-Up

Sugarcane is a kind of grass that grew naturally in India for centuries. People chewed it. It had to be eaten while it was fresh because the sweet juice inside dried up. It was not until A.D. 350 or so that farmers in India started drying the juice and breaking it into sugar bits.

Rice and Spice

Remember how you learned to make rangoli designs? Now, try going a step further. Rangoli is also sometimes made with rice flour and other materials.

Materials Needed
- Construction paper
- Pencil
- Rice flour or wheat flour
- Transparent glue
- Brush (optional)
- Colored spices

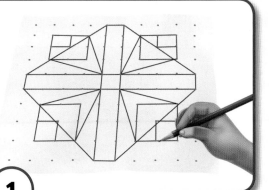

1 Start the same way you did with your first rangoli drawing. Make a grid of pencil dots on the paper, and figure out how you want your lines to look.

2 Practice letting a handful of flour dribble between your fingers onto some scrap paper. Next, decide which sections of your design will be white with flour.

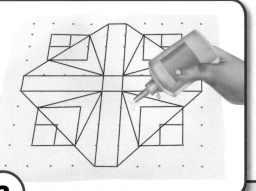

3 Think about keeping the white "even" in the design. Glue those sections, add the flour, and tip the paper to get rid of any extra flour.

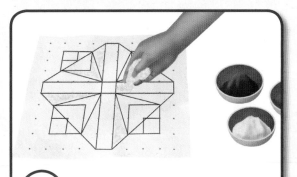

4 "Color" other parts of the design with the glue and spices. Keep the color even. Then, let the glue, and your masterpiece, dry.

27

Wrap It Up

Starting long ago, the way to dress was to wear wraps. Women in India have long dressed in **saris**. Those are long pieces of cloth that can be wrapped in different ways. A sari can be worn as a skirt. The open end can be thrown over a shoulder. A sari can even be wrapped around the legs to wear as pants. The **dhoti** is a strip of material a man can wear around the waist and legs.

Needles for sewing were found in the Indus valley ruins. The first mention of weaving is found in the Vedas.

Gold Standard

As the people of India met with people from elsewhere, they began wearing **tunics** as well. Women started wearing their saris over a top called a **choli**. Many men wore turbans. Everyone who could wore gold. The metal was believed to make things pure.

The choli has short sleeves and is worn like an undershirt.

29

Fine Fabric

The sari is a timeless design. The typical sari is five to six yards of fabric, but some saris are as long as nine yards. Since ancient times, wearing a white sari meant the person was in mourning. Young women tended to wear bright colors. Most people wore saris made of cotton, but rich people had silk saris.

The red dot is called a bindi.

Close-Up

Many people put flowers in their hair for further decoration. They drew with kohl around the eyes. To finish the look, many women added a red dot in the middle of their foreheads. Some people call it the "third eye." That spot was believed to be where wisdom sits.

So Sari!

The silk sari was high fashion for ancient women and remains popular in Indian culture to this day. To see how a sari stays together, try using a doll for a model.

Materials Needed
- Small doll in a standing position
- Measuring tape
- Strip of cloth or wide ribbon

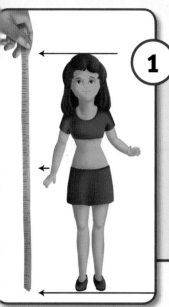

1 First, measure the height of your doll and divide it in half. This is how wide the cloth or ribbon should be.

2 Start by holding the corner of the cloth near the doll's right hip and wrap around the waist once, as you would a beach towel. Wrap it one more time, and then tuck the top of the cloth into itself to hold it in place.

3 Now wrap the cloth around the waist again. This time, when you get back to the right hip, you will begin making a series of small vertical folds called pleats. Keep the spacing even across the front. When you reach the left hip, tuck the tops of the pleats into the waistband of the sari to hold them in place.

4 Now, wrap the cloth one more time around the back. This time, come back around, and pull the cloth under the right arm and across the chest. Drape some extra cloth over the left shoulder and down the back. Now, cut the cloth. The sari is done!

Polished Look

During the Mauryan dynasty, artists perfected the art of wood polishing. They were able to make wood look like mirrors. The artists then turned those same skills to stone polishing. Their larger art pieces were made for the temples. Under the influence of Greek artists, they made beautiful statues of religious figures in black stone.

The public art mainly had religious themes.

Art for the Ages

In early times, most art was tied to beliefs and religion. The artists of the region worked with stone, metals, and other materials. The art showed elements of nature, such as trees. It also featured people but as part of something larger. The artists tried to show larger truths about life on Earth.

The craftspeople of India have long made beautiful jewelry.

Painted pottery is a relatively new development. The early pottery did not even have a glaze.

Dance of Life

Dance was part of worship. Special dance forms developed in different areas over time. Music had regional differences as well. The North and the South ended up with distinct sounds. It is difficult to assign a beginning to any one kind of performance. Yet it is clear the roots of today's traditional music flowed from the first folk musicians, who performed at festivals, along with the dancers.

When the Hindu god Shiva dances, the dance stands for birth and death, creativity and destruction. When the Vedas were first written, Shiva was known as Rudra.

Close-Up

In the old times, drums were the main instruments. The Vedas spoke of musicians playing flutes and drums while priests sang along. Musicians built many types of instruments, such as the **veena** and **sitar**. Some of the instruments were unique to certain areas.

Feeling Plucky

One of the main sounds used in Indian music comes from a group of plucked string instruments called zithers. You can make your own basic zither in no time at all.

2 Tape one pencil straight across the top of the box, near one of the short edges.

1 Make sure the box is totally empty, and remove any plastic that may be covering any part of the opening in the box top.

3 Tape the other pencil at an angle near the opposite edge. This will serve as the "bridge" that will help make the sounds.

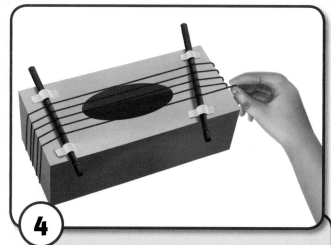

4 Stretch the rubber bands around the box so they rest on top of the pencils and over the opening. Each one should produce a different note. You can tune them by adjusting them back and forth along the angled pencil.

Good Sports

From the start, being physically fit was considered important. Games that developed strength and speed were central to the culture. Leaders were expected to be good at chariot racing and archery. They worked at swimming, wrestling, and hunting. Buddha was thought to be good at all those things.

Buddha was said to be an excellent archer. He was also good at an ancient sport that was like hammer throwing.

Fighting Form

Martial arts originated in south Asia. In one early form of fighting, the players struck, kicked, and pulled at one another. They used swords and knives. The control of breathing as a means of strength was also studied and advanced in India. Physical perfection had an important role in Hindu and Buddhist traditions.

In India, physical fitness has long been considered part of spiritual fitness.

The Players

Many familiar board games, such as chess and chutes and ladders, were developed in south Asia. It is hard to pin down the dates and facts, however. It is harder than winning chess in four moves! What is clear is that the game of chess played now is similar to but different from the original game. The rules changed as the game was shared around the world.

Chess grew out of a game called chaturanga. The exact rules of that game are no longer known.

Close-Up

Playing cards were also developed in India. The royals of India were especially fond of card games. The highest card was a king on horseback. The second highest was a general. Then there were various lords, including a king of the forest.

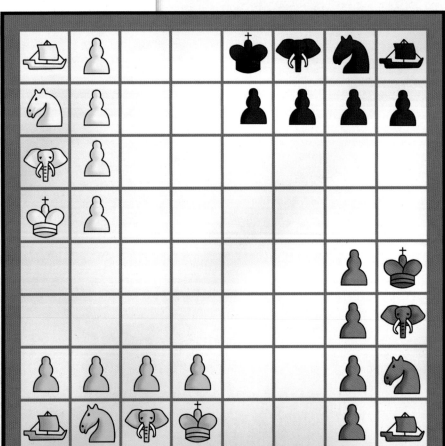

King You

Some people say the people of India invented chess. We may never know for sure if that is true, but we do know that millions of people enjoy the modern version. To see why, follow these moves and start playing.

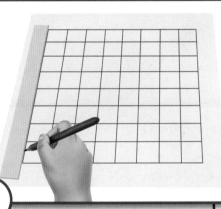

1 Using the ruler, draw a grid of 2-inch squares, with eight rows and eight columns, on the poster board.

2 Color every other square black. The result should look like what is pictured here.

3 Now, cut 32 squares, each 1 inch tall and wide, from another section of poster board. These will be your pieces.

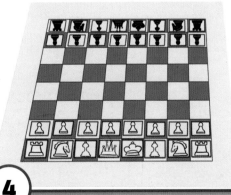

4 Chess is played between two sides, white and black. For each side you will need the following 16 pieces: eight pawns, two knights, two rooks, two bishops, one queen, and one king. Label the pieces you cut out accordingly, and color one set.

Write Ways

The foundation of Hindu study was the Vedas. The information in them was passed from teller to teller for thousands of years. Some of the knowledge was protected by particular families. The actual texts were written over a long span of time as well. In the end, there were four Vedas, and each had four main parts.

The Upanishads were added to the earlier Vedas. The Upanishads discuss how the soul can find truth.

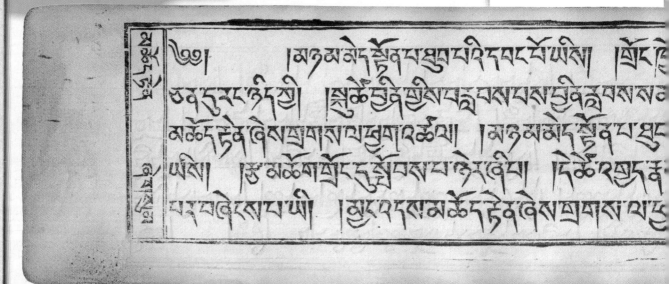

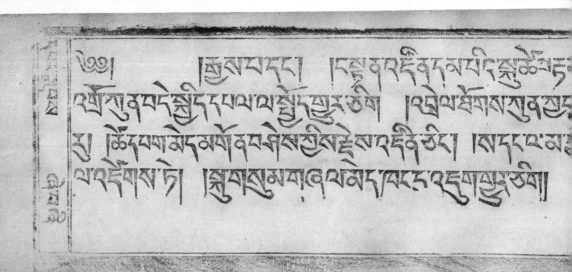

The Script

The official language was Sanskrit. It is older than both Latin and Greek. To understand Sanskrit, it is important to say the words the right way. **Sanskrit** has dozens of words for the concept of love alone. The literature that people studied included poems and dramas. It also passed along technical knowledge, such as what was known about medicine.

In mythology, a figure named Krishna or Vyasa is the scribe of the Vedas.

Subject Matters

Simple facts were not central to learning. In ancient India, the main subject of education was how the mind worked. The teachers believed that how a mind worked was more important than the body of knowledge a person had at any one time. They believed that a ready mind would do its work.

In the beginning, education was just for the upper castes, but it was eventually opened to all.

Close-Up

In early India, when a child was sent to school, he or she was truly sent. The school system was residential. The students lived at the teacher's home or in temples or community centers. The students begged on the streets to get what was needed to support the classes.

The Vedas include verses that can be chanted.

Ink in the Sink

To write their texts before there were paper and pens, the scribes used ink made from soot and natural dyes. Now, you can make your own India ink. Try writing on leaves or cloth, as they did!

Materials Needed
- Small jar
- ½ cup blackberries
- Strainer
- ½ teaspoon vinegar
- ½ teaspoon salt
- Cotton swab
- Paper

1 Work in a sink. Push the berries through the strainer into the jar to get pure juice. Try to avoid getting bits of seeds and pulp.

2 Add the vinegar. This will hold the color.

3 Add the salt. This will preserve the ink.

4 Try using the swab to write with your ink. Just try not to get any on your clothes. It stains!

Glossary

bronze—metal made of copper, tin, and other elements

Buddhism—religion that grew from the teachings of a man called Buddha

burial mounds—mounds of dirt and stone raised over graves

caste system—division of society based on wealth, rank, and occupation

choli—short blouse with short sleeves

citadels—walled fortresses or strongholds

dhoti—cloth that covers the hip area

dynasty—succession of rulers from one family

ghee—butter that has been heated so the fattest parts can be removed

granaries—storehouses for grain

hemp—tall plant with fibers that are used to make materials

Hinduism—religion that grew out of India and belief in divine laws

Iron Age—period of human history characterized by the use of iron tools

Jainism—religion that teaches how to free the soul through faith and conduct

jatis—communities people are born into

monasteries—houses for people in religious establishments

monsoons—periodic winds that bring heavy rainfall

plumb bob—line that has a weight and shows when something is vertical

rangoli—design or ancient form of artwork thought to bring luck

sanctuaries—sacred places that offer a form of protection

Sanskrit—official language of ancient India

saris—wrap dresses or gowns

sitar—stringed instrument that resembles a guitar

standard weights—solids used as a standard for comparison and measurement

stupas—mound-like structures that contain relics of Buddhism or Jainism

subcontinent—landmass that is part of a continent but considered independent

textiles—woven cloths

tributaries—streams that flow to larger streams or bodies of water

tunics—garments that resemble long T-shirts

Vedas—sacred writings of Hinduism

veena—stringed instrument that resembles a harp

vegetarian—having to do with food that does not include meat, fish, or poultry

For Further Information

Books

Cut and Make Festival Masks from India. R. M. Lehri. (Dover Publications, 2001)

Incredible India. Lisa Thompson. (Coughlan Publishing, 2006)

Jahanara: Princess of Princesses, India, 1627. Kathryn Lasky. (Scholastic, 2002)

Taj Mahal. Elizabeth Mann. (Mikaya Press, 2008)

Websites

Indian Child: Ancient India Tales
http://www.indianchild.com/ancient_india_tales.htm

Reading Indian poetry and other literature is another way to explore India. The makers of this site have gathered classic Indian stories, such as "The Legend of the Rice."

India Past and Present
http://india.mrdonn.org/

At this student-friendly site, curious students can find out more about the mysterious Indus valley civilization and the developments that followed its disappearance.

Kidipede: Ancient India
http://www.historyforkids.org/learn/india/

The Kidipede site about ancient India covers topics of historical and everyday interest and helps readers better understand India's fascinating culture.

Social Studies for Kids: Ancient India
http://www.socialstudiesforkids.com/subjects/ancientindia.htm

This site discusses trade between ancient India and the Roman Empire, along with other aspects of India's long history and colorful, complicated culture.

Publisher's note to educators and parents: Our editors have carefully reviewed these websites to ensure that they are suitable for students. Many websites change frequently, however, and we cannot guarantee that a site's future contents will continue to meet our high standards of quality and educational value. Be advised that students should be closely supervised whenever they access the Internet.

Index

Things to Think About and Do

Final Word

In India, there is a story about a king who wanted to teach his sons to live wisely. The king brought them a teacher, who taught the boys 87 stories, which contained all the lessons they needed to know.

Some of the teacher's stories are about friendship. Others are about thinking things through before acting. Many of them teach lessons about work and money. In one, there are three fish in a lake. One fish believes in fate. The second believes he can solve any problem because he is smart. The third one is the wise one. He thinks long and hard before acting.

Try It!

Imagine those three fish or another trio of animals. Write a story in which the first two animals learn a lesson.